of
Greece

BIRDS
of
GREECE

by George Sfikas

EFSTATHIADIS GROUP

Efstathiadis Group S.A.
Agiou Athanasiou Street,
GR - 145 65 Anixi, Attikis

ISBN 960 226 199 4

Printed and bound in Greece by Efstathiadis Group S.A.

Contents

CORMORANT: *A large bird, measuring about 90 centimetres, the cormorant nests high in trees bordering on rivers or lakes, and feeds exclusively on fish which it catches by diving right into the water. It is endemic to Northern Greece, but migrates to Southern Greece for the winter.*

ΚΟΡΜΟΡΑΝΟΣ: *Πουλί μεγάλο μήκους περίπου 90 ἑκ. Φωλιάζει πάνω στά δένδρα τῶν ποταμῶν καί τῶν λιμνῶν καί τρέφεται ἀποκλειστικά μέ ψάρια πού τά πιάνει βουτώντας στό νερό. Στήν Νότια Ἑλλάδα κατεβαίνει τόν χειμώνα. Στή Βόρεια εἶναι ἐνδημικός.*

GRAND CORMORAN: *Grand oiseau, mesurant environ 90 cm. Il fait son nid sur les arbres des rivières et des lacs et se nourrit exclusivement de poissons qu'il attrape en plongeant. Au sud de la Grèce il descend seulement pour y passer l'hiver. Au nord il vit pendant toute l'année.*

KORMORAN: *Ein großer Vogel von rd. 90 cm Länge. Er baut sein Nest auf den Bäumen an den Flüssen und Seen und nährt sich ausschließlich von Fischen, die er - ins Wasser tauchend - fängt. Er zieht im November nach Griechenland. Im Norden ist er ein Zugvogel.*

CORMORANO: *Grosso uccello della lunghezza di circa 90 centimetri. Nidifica sugli alberi lungo le rive dei fiumi e dei laghi cacciando i pesci di cui si nutre. Nella Grecia meridionale fa la sua apparizione d'inverno. Nella Grecia settentrionale è endemico.*

SKARV, KORMORAN: *En stor fågel, som mäter ungefär 90 cm, bygger sitt bo i träden vid floder och sjöar och dess föda består uteslutande av fiskar, som den fångar genom att dyka ner i vattnet. Den flyttar till södra Grekland på vintern. I norr är den inhemsk.*

AALSCHOLVER: *Een grote, ongeveer 90 cm. lange vogel, die boven in bomen bij rivieren nestelt en zich uitsluitend met vis voedt, die hij, al duikend in het water, vangt. 's Winters trekt hij naar Zuid-Griekenland. In Noord-Griekenland is hij inheems.*

1. Phalacrocorax carbo.

体長90cmの大きな鳥で、川や湖との境の木の上に高く巣を作り、専ら水に飛びこん でつかまえた魚をエサとする。　北部ギリシャ特有の鳥であるが、冬には南部ギリシャへ 渡る。

PURPLE HERON: A large bird measuring up to 80 centimetres from beak to tail. It summers in the lake regions and river deltas of Northern Greece, having migrated from Africa. It rears its young in the reeds where it builds nest from twigs and long grasses.

ΠΟΡΦΥΡΟΤΣΙΚΝΙΑΣ: Μεγάλο πουλί πού τό μῆκος του φθάνει τά 80 ἑκ. ἀπό τό ράμφος ὥς τήν οὐρά. Ζεῖ στίς λίμνες καί στά δέλτα τῶν ποταμῶν τῆς Β. ᾽Ελλάδας ὅπου ἔρχεται κάθε καλοκαίρι ἀπό τήν ᾽Αφρική. Φωλιάζει στίς καλαμιές.

HERON POUPRRE: Grand oiseau échassier dont la longueur atteint 80 cm. du bec à la queue. Il vient d'Afrique pour passer l'été au nord de la Grèce près des lacs et des deltas des rivières, où il fait son nid dans les roseaux.

PUR PURREIHER: Ein großer Vogel, dessen Länge 80 cm vom Schnabel bis zum Schwanz erreichen kann. Er lebt in Seen und im Delta nordgriechischer Flüsse, wo er jeden Sommer aus Afrika kommt. Er baut sein Nest im Schilfrohr.

AIRONE ROSSO: Grosso uccello la cui lunghezza raggiuge gli ottanta centimetri, calcolando dalla coda fino ai becco lungo. Vive sulle rive dei laghi e sulle foci dei fiumi della Grecia settentrionale over fa la sua apparizione nella stagione estiva migrando dall'Africa. Nidifica nei canneti.

PURPUR HÄGER: Stor fågel, vars längd når upp till 80 cm från näbben till stjärten. Den lever i sjöar och floddeltor i norra Grekland, dit den kommer varje sommar från Afrika. Bygger bon i vassen.

PURPERREIGER (Grieks: Porfyrotkniás): Een grote vogel, die van snavel tot staart tot 80 cm. lang wordt. Hij leeft bij plassen en rivierdelta's in Noord-Griekenland, waar hij elke zomer vanuit Afrika komt. Hij nestelt in het riet.

2. Ardea
purpurea.

ムラサキサギ

体長80cmにも及ぶ大きな鳥。　夏にアフリカより渡ってきて、北部ギリシャの湖沼
地帯や三角洲地帯に棲息する。　葦の中に小枝や長い草を集めて巣を作りひなを育
てる。

WHITE STORK: A very large bird measuring 102 centimetres from beak to tail. It comes to Greece in the summer and constructs its nests on rooftops, in belfries, on power poles, in old ruins or in tall isolated tress. It feeds on various accuatic animals which it catches in the shallows of lakes, rivers or swamps.

ΑΣΠΡΟΠΕΛΑΡΓΟΣ: Πουλί μεγάλο σέ μῆκος 102 ἑκ. ἀπό τό ράμφος ὥς τήν οὐρά. Στήν Ἑλλάδα ἔρχεται τό καλοκαίρι καί φτιάχνει τίς φωλιές του στά καμπαναριά, στίς κολῶνες τοῦ ἠλεκτρικοῦ, σέ παλιά ἐρείπια ἤ σέ ἀπομονωμένα δένδρα. Τρέφεται μέ διάφορα ὑδρόβια ζῶα πού πιάνει στά ρηχά τῶν λιμνῶν, τῶν ποταμῶν καί τῶν τελμάτων.

CIGOGNE BLANCHE: Grand oiseau, mesurant 102 cm. du bec à la queue. En Grèce il vient pour l'été et construit son nid sur les clochers, les poteaux télégraphiques, les vieilles ruines ou les arbres isolés. La cigogne se nourrit d'animaux aquatiques qu'elle attrape dans les eaux basses des lacs et dans les marécages.

WEISSER STORCH: Ein großer Vogel mit einer Gesamtlänge (vom Schnabel bis zum Schwanz) von 102 cm. Nach Griechenland kommt er im Sommer und baut sein Nest auf den Kirchtürmen, den Stromleitungsmasten, in alten Ruinen oder auf abseits stehenden Bäumen. Er nährt sich von verschiedenen Wassertieren, die er in den seichten Gewässern der Seen, Flüsse und Sümpfe fängt.

CICOGNA BIANCA: Grosso uccello che raggiunge, calcolando dalla coda al becco, i 102 centimetri. In Grecia migra durante la stagione estiva e nidifica sui campanili, sui pali elettrici, su vecchie costruzioni cadute in rovina, su alberi solitari. Si nutre di piccoli mammiferi, rane, pesci serpi, insetti, ecc. che caccia tra le acque basse dei laghi, dei fiumi e delle zone paludose.

VIT STORK: En stor fågel med en längd av 102 cm från näbben till stjärten. Till Grekland kommer den på sommaren och bygger sina bon i klockstaplar, elektriska stolpar, gamla ruiner eller avsides växande träd. Den föder sig på olika vattendjur, som den fångar vid sjöstränderna, vid floderna och träsken.

(WITTE) OOIEVAAR: Een grote vogel, 102 cm. lang van snavel tot staart. Hij trekt in de zomer naar Griekenland en bouwt zijn nest op kerktorens, electriciteitspalen, oude ruᵢnes of alleenstaande bomen. Zijn voedsel bestaat uit verschillende waterdieren, die hij in ondiepe gedeelten van meren, rivieren en moerassen vangt.

3. Ciconia
ciconia.

シュバシコウヅル

体長102cmにも及ぶ大きな鳥。　夏にギリシャに渡ってきて、教会の塔の上、送電塔、
廃虚、高い孤立した木の上等に巣を作る。　湖や川、沼の浅瀬にいる水棲動物
を エサとする。

MALLARD: The most common of wild ducks and the progenitor of the domestic duck. Only the male of the species is brightly coloured; the female is a dull chestnut-grey with darker markings. 58 centimetres in length, the mallard is the largest dabbling duck. It nests on lake shores, and lives in Greece throughout the year.

ΠΡΑΣΙΝΟΚΕΦΑΛΗ ΠΑΠΙΑ: Ἡ πιό κοινή ἀπ' ὅλες τίς ἀγριόπαπιες καί πρόγονος τῆς ἥμερης πάπιας. Μόνο τό ἀρσενικο ἔχει λαμπερά χρώματα. Τό θηλυκό εἶναι μονόχρωμο σταχτοκαστανό μέ βοῦλες πιό σκοῦρες. Φωλιάζει στίς λίμνες. Ζεῖ στήν Ἑλλάδα ὅλον τόν χρόνο.

CANARD COL-VERT: Le plus commun de tous les canards, et aïeul du canard domestique. Seul le mâle a des couleurs brillantes. La femelle est uniformément marron cendré avec des tâches plus foncées. Cet oiseau fait son nid près des lacs. Il vit en Grèce pendant toute l'année.

STOCKENTE: Die am weitest verbreitete Wildente, die zugleich ein Vorläufer der zahmen Ente ist. Nur das männliche Tier besitzt leuchtende Farben. Das weibliche Tier ist einfarbig aschbran mit dunkleren Flecken. Sie baut ihr Nest an Seen. In Griechenland lebt sie das ganze Jahr über.

ANATRA O GERMANO REALE: La più comune tra la anatre selvatiche e l'antenata delle anatre domestiche. Unicamente il maschio ha il piumaggio di colori sgargianti. La femmina è fornita di un piumaggio monocolore cenere scuro con grosse macchie più scure. Nidifica sui laghi. Vive stabilmente in Grecia.

GRÄSAND: Den vanligaste av alla vildänder och förfader till den tama anden. Det är endast hanen som har lysande färger. Honan är enfärgad grå-brun med mörkare fläckar. Den bygger sitt bo vid sjöar. Lever i Grekland under hela året.

WILDE EEND: De gewoonste van alle wilde eenden en de voorouder van de tamme eend. Alleen het mannetj heeft fraaie kleuren. Het wijfje is egaal asbruin met donkerder plekken. Hij nestelt aan meeroevers en leeft het gehele jaar in Griekenland.

**4. Anas
platyrhynchos.**

マガモ

最もよく見られる野ガモの種類で、アヒルの原種。 明るい色はオスだけで、メスは
こいもようを浮かべた暗い茶灰色をしている。 体長は58cmで、カモの類では一番
大きい。 湖岸に巣を作り、四季を通じてギリシャに見られる。

TEAL: A beautiful wild duck measuring 35 centimetes, the teal spends only the winter months in Greece and then, with the coming of spring, flies to more northern climes for its breeding season. The female is a much plainer speckled brown with only a green stipe on its wing.

KIPKIPI: Ὡραία ἀγριόπαπια μήκους 35 ἑκ. Στήν Ἑλλάδα κατεβαίνει μόνο γιά νά ξεχειμωνιάσει στίς λίμνες καί στίς καλαμιές. Τήν ἄνοιξη φεύγει γιά τίς βορειότερες χῶρες ὅπου ἀναπαράγεται.

CRECELLE D'HIVER: Beau canard sauvage long de 35 cm; en Grèce, il descend seulement pour y passer l'hiver près des lacs aù milieu des roseaux. Au printemps, il s'envole vers les pays du nord où il se reproduit.

KRICKENTE: Eine schöne Wildentenart mit einer Länge von 35 cm. Nach Griechenland zieht sie nur, um hier an den Seen und im Schilf zu überwintern. Im Frühling wandert sie in die nördlichen Länder, wo sie sich vermehrt.

RAGANELLA: Bella anatra selvatica di una lunghezza di trentacinque centimetri. Migra in Grecia per svernare sui laghi e nei canneti. Non appena giunta la primavera migra verso regioni più settentrionali ove depone le uova per la riproduzione.

KRICKA: En vacker vildand, ungefär 35 cm lång. Till Grekland kommer den bara ner för att övervintra vid sjöar och i vassen. På våren flyttar den upp till nordligare länder, där den förökar sig.

WINTERTALING: Een mooie wilde eend, 35cm. lang. Hij komt naar Griekenland alleen om in het riet langs meren en plassen te overwinteren. In de lente trekt hij weg naar noordelijker streken, waar hij zich voortplant.

5. Anas crecca.

カルガモ

体長35cmの美しい野ガモ．　冬季にのみギリシャに棲息し　春の到来と共に卵をか
えすために北の地へ移る．　メスはまだらの茶で，羽に緑の線があるだけの地味な
姿をしている．

GOSHAWK: *A carnivorous bird of prey, the goshawk measures 48-61 centimetres. The male and female of the species are very similar in appearance, but the female is larger in size; the younger birds are uniform in colour. The species lives in Greece throughout the year.*

ΔΙΠΛΟΣΑΙΝΟ: *Ὡραῖο ἁρπακτικό μήκους 48-61 ἑκ. Ἀρσενικό καί θηλυκό μοιάζουν ἀλλά τό θηλυκό εἶναι πιό μεγάλο. Τά νεαρά ἔχουν ὁμοιόμορφο χρῶμα. Τό Διπλοσάινο ζεῖ στήν Ἑλλάδα ὅλο τόν χρόνο.*

AUTOUR DES PALOMPES: *Beau rapace mesurant entre 48 et 61 cm. Mâle et femelle se ressemblent mais la femelle est plus grande. Les jeunes oiseaux sont de couleur plus unie. L'autour des palompes vit en Grèce pendant toute l'année.*

HABICHT: *Ein schöner Raubvogel von 48-61 cm Länge. Das männliche und weibliche Tier sind einander ähnlich, jedoch ist das weibliche größer. Die jungen Tiere besitzen eine gleichmäßigere und einheitlichere Farbzeichnung. Der Habicht lebt in Griechenland das ganze Jahr über.*

ASTORE: *Bell'uccello rapace della lunghezza approssimativa di 48-61 centimetri. Il maschio e la femmina si assomigliano, tuttavia la femmina è di maggiori dimensioni. Nei giovani astori l'uniformità del colore nel piumaggio è più marcata. Vive per tutto l'anno in Grecia.*

DUVHÖK: *En vacker rovfågel, 48 cm–61 cm lång. Hanen och honan liknar varandra, men honan är större. De unga har en jämnare färg. Duvhöken lever i Grekland hela året runt.*

HAVIK: *Een fraaie roofvogel, tot 61 cm. lang. Het mannetje en het wijfje lijken op elkaar, maar het wijfje is groter. De jongen zijn meer egaal van kleur. De havik verblijft her gehele jaar in Griekenland.*

**6. Accipiter
gentilis.**

オオタカ

体長48-61cmの食肉性の鳥。 オス・メスよく似ており。特に若鳥のうちは同じ色をし
ているが。メスの方が大きい。 四季を通じてギリシャに棲息する。

PEREGRINE FALCON: This is the most familiar of the European hawks, measuring from 38 to 48 centimetres. Pictured here is a young bird, chestnut in colour. The mature birds have dark grey backs and almost pure white undersides with dark markings. The peregrine feeds on smaller birds, striking in midair as the prey takes flight, and plunging down through the air with terrific speed and accuracy.

ΠΕΤΡΙΤΗΣ: Τό πιό γνωστό γεράκι τῆς Εὐρώπης. Ἔχει μῆκος 38-48 ἑκ. Τό πουλί τῆς εἰκόνας εἶναι ἕνα νεαρό ἄτομο μέ χρῶμα καστανό. Τά ἐνήλικα ἄτομα ἔχουν χρῶμα σταχτί σκοῦρο ἀπό πάνω καί σχεδόν λευκό μέ σκοῦρες βοῦλες ἀπό κάτω. Ὁ πετρίτης τρέφεται μέ πουλιά, πού τά πιάνει στόν ἀέρα καθώς πετοῦν, ὁρμώντας μέ καταπληκτική ταχύτητα.

FAUCON PELERIN: Le faucon plus connu d'Europe, mesurant entre 38 et 48 cm. L'oiseau de l'image ci-contre est un jeune faucon de couleur brune. Les adultes sont gris cendrée foncé sur le dos et presque blanc avec des tâches noires sur le ventre. Le faucon pélerin se nourrit d'oiseaux qu'il attrape au vol en fon$ant sur eux avec grande rapidité.

WANDERFALKE: Die bekannteste europäische Falkenart. Seine Länge beträgt 38-48 cm. Der abgebildete Vogel ist ein Jungtier von kastanienbrauner Farbe. Die erwachsenen Tiere haben eine dunkle aschgraue Färbung oben und eine fast weiße mit dunklen Flecken auf der Unterseite. Der Wanderfalke nährt sich von Vögeln, die er im Fluge fängt, wobei er mit erstaunlicher Geschwindigkeit seine Beute faßt.

FALCO PELLEGRINO: Il falco più noto in Europa. La sua lunghezza varia da 38 a 48 centimetri. Il falco raffigurato nell'illustrazione è un giovane esemplare di colore castano. Gli hanno il piumaggio cenere adulti scuro nella parte superiore, mentre quella inferiore bèiancastra macchiata di chiazze scure. Si nutre di uccelli che riesce ad artigliare volando, assalendo la sua preda con sorprendente velocità.

PILGRIMSFALK: Den mest kända falken i Europa. Den är 38-48 cm lång. Fågeln på bilden är en unge i brun färg. De vuxna fåglarna har en mörkgrå färg på översidan och nästan vit med mörka fläckar på undersidan. Pilgrimsfalken föder sig på fåglar, som den griper i luften, sedan den dykt ner på den med fruktansvärd hastighet.

SLECHTVALK: De meest bekende valk van Europa. Hij heeft een lengte van 38-48 cm. De vogel op de afbeelding is een jong exemplaar, kastanjebruin van kleur. De volwassen exemplaren zijn aan de bovenkant donkergrijs en van onder bijna wit met donkere plekken. De slechtvalk voedt zich met vogels, die hij in de lucht vangt, waarbij hij zich met verbazingwekkende snelheid op hen stort.

7. Falco
peregrinus.

ハヤブサ

ヨーロッパのタカの類では最もなじみ深い鳥で、体長は38-48cm。　写真は若鳥で
褐色をしている。　成鳥になると、背中がこい灰色になり、腹はこいもようを浮かべた純
白色になる。　猛烈なスピードで目標めがけて的確に急降下し、飛行中の小さい鳥を
襲ってエサにする。

OYSTERCATCHER: The habitant of this bird is the seashore, where it feeds on shellfish and other shore creatures. It constructs its nest in the sand. Oystercatchers, measuring 43 centimetres, winter in Southern Greece and summer in the North.

ΣΤΡΕΙΔΟΦΑΓΟΣ: Πουλί πού ζεῖ στίς παραλίες καί τρέφεται μέ ἀχιβάδες κι ἄλλα ζῷα τῶν ἀκτῶν. Τή φωλιά του τή φτιάχνει στήν ἄμμο. Στήν Ν. ΄Ελλάδα ἔρχεται τόν χειμώνα ἐνῶ στή Βόρεια τό καλοκαίρι. Τό μῆκος του εἶναι 43 ἑκ.

HUITRIER PIE: Oiseau qui vit au bord de la mer et se nourrit d'hu"tres et autres mollusques marins. Il fait son nid dans le sable. Il vit au sud de la Grèce pendant l'hiver et au nord pendant l'été. Il mesure 43 cm.

AUSTERNFISCHER: Ein an den Küsten lebender Vogel, der sich von Muscheln und anderen an den Küsten lebenden Tieren ernährt. Sein Nest baut er im Sand. Nach Südgriechenland kommt er im Winter während er im Sommer nach Norden zieht. Seine Länge beträgt 43 cm.

BECCACCIA DI MARE: Vive lungo le rive e si nutre di ostriche e di altri molluschi. Si costruisce il nido nella sabbia. Nella Grecia meridionale fa la sua apparizione in inverno, mentre in quella settentrionale in estate. La sua lunghezza raggiunge i 43 centimetri.

STRANDSKATA: En fågel som lever vid stränderna och föder sig på snäckor och andra stranddjur. De bygger sina bon i sanden. Den flyttar ner till södra Grekland på vintern, från sommarvistelsen i norr. Dess längd är omkring 43 cm.

SCHOLEKSTER: Een vogel van de zeekust, die zich voedt met schelpdieren en andere dieren van het kustgebied. Hij bouwt zijn nest in het zand. 's Winters trekt hij naar Zuid-Griekenland, 's zomers naar het Noorden. Lengte 45 cm.

8. Haematopus ostralegus.

ミヤコドリ

海岸に棲息し、貝など浜辺の生物をエサにする。　砂の中に巣を作る。　体長43cm.
冬を南部ギリシャで、夏を北部ギリシャで過ごす。

HERRING GULL: This is the commonest of the local gulls. It is found everywhere along the mainland coast and on the islands. In winter it flies deep inland to river and lake regions. The young are of plain grey to chestnut colour. Herring gulls feed on fish and measure 56 centimetres.

ΑΣΗΜΟΓΛΑΡΟΣ: Είναι ό πιό κοινός γλάρος τῆς χώρας μας. Ζεῖ παντοῦ στίς ἀκτές καί στά νησιά. Τό χειμώνα μπαίνει βαθιά μέσα στήν ξηρά κατά μῆκος τῶν ποταμῶν καθώς καί σέ μέρη πού ὑπάρχουν λίμνες. Τά νεαρά εἶναι ὁμοιόχρωμα γκριζοκαστανά. Μῆκος 56 ἑκ. Τρέφεται μέ ψάρια.

GOELAND ARGENTE: La plus commune des mouettes de notre pays. On la rencontre aux rivages de la Grèce continentale ainsi qu'aux "les. Pendant l'hiver elle abandonne la vie marine pour les bords des rivières et des lacs. Les jeunes goélands sont de couleur brune unie. L'oiseau adulte mesure 56 cm. et se nourrit de poissons.

SILBERMOVE: Es ist die am verbreitetste Mövenart in Griechenland. Sie lebt überall an den Küsten und auf den Inseln. Im Winter zieht sie tief ins Landesinnere entlang von Flüssen sowie in die Nachbarschaft von Häfen. Die Jungen sind von gleichmäßig graubrauner Farbe. Ihre Länge beträgt 56 cm. Sie nährt sich von Fischen.

GABBIANO REALE: E'il gabbiano più comune che vive in Grecia. Lo si trova dappertutto nelle isole come sulle rive. Durante l'inverno si addentra profondamente nel retroterra cercando rifugio lungo i fiumi e i laghi. I giovani gabbiani hanno il piumaggio uniforme di un colore grigio-castano. Raggiunge la lunghezza di 56 centimetri.

GRÅTRUT: Det är den vanligaste måsen i Grekland. Den finns överallt vid kuster och på öar. På vintern flyttar den djupt in i fastlandet längs floderna liksom till platser vid sjöar. De unga har en jämn grå-brun färg. De är 56 cm. lång. Födan utgörs av fisk.

ZILVERMEEUW: De in Griekenland meest voorkomende meeuw. Hij leeft overal langs de kust en op de eilanden. In de winter gaat hij ver het vasteland in langs rivieren en meren. De jongen zijn egaal grijsbruin. Hij voedt zich met vis. Lengte 56 cm.

9. Larus argentatus.

セグロカモメ

ギリシャのカモメの中では最も一般的なもので、本土の海岸沿いや、島のどこにてても見られる。 冬になると内陸の湖川地帯へ渡る。 若鳥は灰色がかった栗色の地味な姿をしている。 体長56cm. 魚をエサとする。

LITTLE TERN: A lovely bird, measuring 24 centimetres, the little tern migrates to Greece from the south every summer, and resides along the coasts where it fishes by diving for its prey.

ΝΑΝΟΓΛΑΡΟΣ: "Όμορφο πουλί μήκους 24 έκ. "Ερχεται στήν 'Ελλάδα άπό τόν νότο κάθε καλοκαίρι καί ζεῖ στίς ἀκτές τῆς θάλασσας πετώντας καί ψαρεύοντας μέ βουτιές.

STERNE NAINE: Joli oiseau mesurant 24 cm. Il vient au sud de la Grèce tous les été et vit au bord de la mer volant et plongeant pour pêcher.

ZWERGSEESCHWALBE: Ein schöner Vogel von 24 cm Länge. Er kommt jeden Sommer aus dem Norden nach Griechenland und lebt an den Meeresküsten, wo er nach Fischen taucht.

STERNA: Bell'uccello della lunghezza di 24 centimetri. Raggiunge la Grecia in estate, venendo da contrade meridionali. Vive lungo le rive del mare nutrendosi di pesci che riesce a pescare tuffandosi nelle acque.

SMÅTÄRNA: En vacker fågel, 24 cm lång. Den kommer varje sommar till Grekland ifrån Söder och lever vid havsstränderna, där den flyger och fiskar med djupdykningar.

DWERGSTERN: Een fraaie, 24 cm. lange vogel, die elke zomer uit het Zuiden naar Griekenland komt en aan de kust leeft, waar hij al vliegend en duikend vis vangt.

**10. Sterna
albifrons.**

コアジサシ

体長24cmの かわいらしい鳥。　毎年夏に なると南から ギリシャへ 渡ってきて 海岸地
帯に 棲息する。　水に とびこんで つかまえた 魚を エサとする。

WOOD PIGEON: *This is the largest of the Greek pigeons, measuring about 41 centimetres. It is endemic to Greece. In summer it nests in mountain woodlands and in winter in afforested areas at lower altitudes.*

ΦΑΣΣΑ: *Τό μεγαλύτερο ἀπό τά ἑλληνικά περιστέρια μήκους 41 ἑκ. περίπου. Στήν Ἑλλάδα εἶναι ἐνδημικό. Τό καλοκαίρι φωλιάζει στά δάση τῶν βουνῶν ἐνῶ τόν χειμώνα κατεβαίνει σέ δασωμένα μέρη χαμηλοῦ ὑψομέτρου.*

PIGEON RAMIER: *Le plus grand des pigeons grecs mesurant environ 41 cm. En Grèce il est endémique, vivant, pendant l'été, dans les forêts des montagnes et, quand vient l'hiver, descendant vers les côtes boisées de plus basse altitude.*

RINGELTAUBE: *Sie ist die größe griechische Taubenart mit einer Länge von rd. 41 cm. In Griechenland ist sie ein Zugvogel, der im Sommer in den Bergwäldern sein Nest baut, während er im Winter zu tiefergelegenen Wäldern umwechselt.*

COLOMBO (PALOMBO): *Il maggiore dei colombi viventi in Grecia. Raggiunge una lunghezza di quarantuno centimetri circa. In Grecia è endemico. Durante l'estate nidifica nelle foreste delle regioni montuose, mentre d'inverno preferisce nidificare in zone boscose di minore altitudine.*

RINGDUVA: *Den största av duvorna i Grekland, med en längd på ungefär 41 cm. Den är inhemsk i Grekland. På sommaren bygger den sina bon i bergsskogarna, medan de på vintern flyttar ner till skogar på låg höjd.*

HOUTDUIF: *De grootste van de Griekse duiven, ongeveer 41 cm. lang. In Griekenland is hij inheems. In de zomer nestelt hij in bergwouden, terwijl hij in de zomer afdaalt naar lager gelegen bosrijke streken.*

11. Columba palumpus.

ジュズカケバト

ギリシャのハトの中では最大で，体長41cm．　ギリシャ特有．　夏には山の森林地帯に棲息するが，冬は伯地の森林地帯に移る．

STOCK DOVE: Common in Greece, this bird measures 32 centimetres, and lives in scrubland or in open woodland. It comes down to the milder climate of Southern Greece only during the winter months, being endemic to the northern regions of the country.

ΦΑΣΣΟΠΕΡΙΣΤΕΡΟ: Περιστέρι κοινό στήν Ἑλλάδα. Τό μῆκος του εἶναι 32 ἑκ. Ζεῖ σέ θαμνότοπους καί ἀραιά δάση. Στήν Ν. Ἑλλάδα ἔρχεται μόνο τό χειμώνα. Ἀντίθετα στά βόρεια μέρη τῆς χώρας εἶναι ἐνδημικό.

PIGEON COLOMBIER: Pigeon très commun en Grèce, mesurant 32 cm. Il vit dans les buissons et préfère les terrains peu boisés du nord de la Grèce. Au sud il descend seulement en hiver.

HOHLTAUBE: Eine gewöhnliche Taubenart in Griechenland. Ihre Längebeträgt 32 cm. Sie lebt im Gebüsch und in lichten Wäldern. Nach Südgriechenland kommt sie nur im Winter. In den nördlichen Gegenden des Landes hingegen ist sie ein Zugvogel.

COLOMBO SELVATICO: Colombo comunissimo in Grecia. La sua lunghezza raggiunge i 32 centimetri. Vive in zone cespugliose e in boschi radi. Raggiunge la Grecia meridionale durante l'inverno. Nelle regioni settentrionali del paese vive in stato endemico.

SKOGSDUVA: En vanlig duva i Grekland. Den är 32 cm lång. Lever i buskvegetation och glesa skogar. Till södra Grekland flyttar den bara på vintern. Däremot är den inhemsk i de norra delarna av landet.

HOLENDUIF: Een in Griekenland veel voorkomende duif. Lengte 32 cm. Hij woont in streken met struikgewas en open bossen. Hij trekt alleen in de winter naar Zuid-Griekenland. In de noordelijke streken van het land is hij echter inheems.

**12. Columba
oenas.**

ノバト

ギリシャでは一般的な鳥で, 体長32cm. かん木地帯や広々とした森林地帯に棲息
する. 北部ギリシャ特有の鳥であるが, 冬の間の暖かい時期には南部ギリシャにも渡る.

COLLARED TURTLE DOVE: A small wild dove which measures around 28 centimetres in length. This is a genus of an Asiatic species which has gradually spread through Europe and seems able to adjust to any environment. It makes its nest in isolated trees, even in those found in city parks. Together with the domestic dove, it is a common sight in cities.

ΔΕΚΟΧΤΟΥΡΑ: Μικρό ἀγριοπερίστερο μήκους γύρω στά 28 ἐκ. Εἶναι εἶδος ἀσιατικῆς καταγωγῆς πού σιγά-σιγά ἐξαπλώθηκε στήν Εὐρώπη. Προσαρμόζεται σ' ὁποιοδήποτε περιβάλλον. Κάνει τίς φωλιές του σέ ψηλά ἀπομονωμένα δένδρα ἀκόμα καί στά πάρκα τῶν πόλεων. Τό βλέπουν συχνά μέσα στίς πόλεις μαζί μέ τά ἤμερα περιστέρια.

TOURTERELLE TURQUE: Petite tourterelle sauvage mesurant environ 28 cm., d'une espèce asiatique qui, au cours des siècles, se répandit en Europe. Elle s'adapte à tous les habitats, nichant sur de grands arbres isolés et même dans les jardins publiques. On la rencontre souvent dans les villes, mêlée aux pigeons domestiques.

TURKENTAUBE: Kleine Wildtaube mit einer Länge von rd. 28 cm. Diese Art ist von asiatischer Herkunft, die sich langsam in Europa ausgebreitet hat. Sie paßt sich jeglicher Umgebung an. Ihr Nest baut sie auf hohen einzelstehenden Bäumen, auch in den Parks von Städten. Sie kommt häufig in Städten zusammen mit den zahmen Tauben vor.

COLOMBO SELVATICO: Colombo selvatico di piccole dimensioni di una lunghezza di circa 28 centimetri. E'di origine asiatica. Specie che col passare del tempo si è diffusa anche in Europa. Si adatta a qualsiasi ambiente. Nidifica sulle cime di alberi isolati, nonché nei parchi pubblici cittadini. Non di rado s'incontra nelle città insieme agli altri colombi.

TURKDUVA: En liten vildduva med en längd av ungefär 28 cm. Den har asiatiskt ursprung och bredde undan för undan ut sig i Europa. Den anpassar sig till vilken miljö som helst. Den bygger sitt bo högt uppe i ensliga träd och även i stadsparker. Man ser den ofta i städerna ihop med de tama duvorna.

TURKSE TORTELDUIF: Een kleine wilde duif, ongeveer 28 cm. lang, van Aziatische oorsprong, die zich langzamerhand over Europa verspreid heeft (men ziet hem ook in Nederland). Hij past zich aan elke omgeving aan. Hij nestelt in hoge alleenstaande bomen, en zelfs ook in stadsparken. Men ziet hem vaak in steden samen met tamme duiven.

**13. Streptopelia
decaocto.**

キジバト

体長28cmの小さな野生のハト.　　元々はアジア種であったものが, どんな環境にも
適応できることから, ヨーロッパ中に分布するようになった.　孤立した木を好み, 街の公園
の木の上にすら巣を作る.　　家バトと共に, 街の日常の光景の一部をなしている.

BARN OWL: *A beautiful bird, measuring 35 centimetres and with grey plumage shading to gold at the crest and lighter beige on the underside. It inhabits the northern areas of Greece.*

ΠΕΠΛΟΚΟΥΚΟΥΒΑΓΙΑ: *Ὡραῖο πουλί μήκους 35 ἑκ. καί πτέρωμα σταχτί μέ χρυσαφιές ἀποχρώσεις στή ράχη καί ἀνοιχτό πρός τό μπέζ στήν κοιλια. Στήν Ἑλλάδα ζεῖ μόνο στά βορειότερα μέρη.*

CHOUETTE EFFRAIE: *Bel oiseau, mesurant 35 cm., au plumage gris avec des reflets dorés sur le dos et clair vers le beige sur le ventre. En Grèce, il vient dans les regions du Nord.*

SCHLEIEREULE: *Ein schöner Vogel mit einer Länge von 35 cm. Sein Federkleid ist auf dem Rücken grau mit Goldschattierungen und hellfarbig bis beige auf dem Bauch. In Griechenland kommt sie nur in den nördlicheren Gegenden vor.*

BARBAGIANNI: *Bell'uccello della lunghezza di circa 35 centimetri. Il suo piumaggio è color cenere con sfumature dorate sul dorso. Nel ventre le sfumature sono più chiare. In Grecia vive nelle regioni settentrionali.*

TORNUGGLA: *En vacker fågel, 35 cm lång och gråa fjädrar med guldstänk på ryggen, och beige-ljus på magen. I Grekland finns den bara i de nordligaste delarna.*

KERKUIL: *Een mooie vogel. Lengte 35 cm, Zijn veren zijn grijs met goudkleurige partijen op de rug, en licht-beige op de buik. In Griekenland komt hij alleen in noordelijke streken voor.*

14. Tyto alba.

フクロウ

体長35cmの美しい鳥で. 灰色の羽毛が頸にかけて金色味を帯び. 腹側は明るい
ベージュ色をしている. 北部ギリシャに棲息する.

KINGFISHER: A bird of spectacular electric blue especially in the mating season, commonly found along the banks of rivers and lakes where it feeds of fish. These it spears with its sharp beak as it skims along the surface of the water, then flies to a nearby branch to shallow the catch. It makes its nest by digging a hole in steep shoreline cliffs. It is a year-round inhabitant of Greece. Length: 17 centimetres.

ΑΛΚΥΩΝΑ: Πουλί κοινό στίς ἀκτές, τά ποτάμια καί τίς λίμνες ὅπου ζεῖ τρώγοντας ψάρια. Τά πιάνει μέ τή σουβλερή μύτη του πετώντας ξυστά πάνω στό νερό κι ὕστερα κάθεται σ᾽ ἕνα κλαδί γιά νά τά καταπιεῖ. Φτιάχνει τή φωλιά του σκάβοντας μιά τρύπα στό κάθετο μέρος μιᾶς ἀπόκρημνης ἀκτῆς. Ζεῖ στήν Ἑλλάδα ὅλο τόν χρόνο. Μῆκος 17 ἑκ.

MARTIN-PECHEUR: Oiseau qui se rencontre souvent au bord de la mer, près des rivières et des lacs où il se nourrit de poissons. Il les attrape avec son bec pointu en effleurant a peine la surface de l'eau, et, après, perche sur une branche pour les avaler. Il fait son nid en creusant un trou dans le versant perpendiculaire des falaises. Il vit en Grèce pendant toute l'année. Longueur: 17 cm.

EISVOGEL: Ein Vogel, der an den Flußufern und Seen häufig verbreitet ist, wo er sich von Fischen nährt. Er fängt sie mit seinem spitzen Schnabel, indem er knapp über dem Wasser hinstreicht und sich dann auf einen Ast setzt, um den Fang zu verspeisen. Sein Nest baut er, indem er ein Loch in den Hang einer steil abfallenden Küste gräbt. Er lebt das ganze Jahr über in Griechenland. Seine Länge beträgt 17 cm.

MARTIN PESCATORE: Uccello comunissimo che vive lungo le rive dei fiumi e dei laghi. Si nutre di pesci. Riesce e pescarli grazie al becco acuto che sfiora le acque. Non appena ha la sua preda nel becco, si poggia su una zampa per, tranquillamente, ingoiarla. Nidifica scavando un foro nella parte verticale a precipizio delle rive. Vive in stato endemico in Grecia. Raggiunge la lunghezza di 17 centimetri.

KUNGSFISKARE: En fågel som är vanlig vid stränder, floder och sjöar, där den lever av fisk. Den fångar fisken med sin långa skarpa näbb, då den flyger précis ovanför vattenytan och sätter sig sedan på en gren och äter upp fisken. Den bygger sitt bo genom att gräva ett hål i den vertikala väggen vid en kustbrant. Den stannar i Grekland hela året. Längden är 17 cm.

IJSVOGEL: Een veel aan de en langs rivieren en meren voorkomende vogel. Kust hij voedt zich met vissen die hij, over het water scherende, met zijn spitse snavel vangt, waarna hij zich op een tak zet om hen op te eten. Hij maakt zijn nest door een holte te graven in de loodrechte wand van een steile oever. Hij leeft het gehele jaar in Griekenland. Lengte 17 cm.

15. Alcedo atthis.

カワセミ

川や湖の土手によく見られる鳥で、魚をエサとする。　特に交尾期には、澄きとおった青い色になる。　水面をさっとかすめながら、鋭いくちばしで獲物をつきさすや近くの枝に飛んで行き、つかまえた獲物を飲みこむ。　海岸の断崖に穴を掘って巣を作る。　ギリシャでは四季を通じて見られる。　体長17cm.

ROLLER: A large bird, measuring 30 centimetres and one of the most beautiful found in Europe, which migrates from Africa to Greece in the summer. It constructs its nest in shoreline cliffs, in tree trunks etc., by digging out a large hole.

ΧΑΛΚΟΚΟΥΡΟΥΝΑ: Πουλί μεγάλο σέ μῆκος 30 ἑκ. ἀπό τά πιό ὄμορφα τῆς Εὐρώπης. Στήν ῾Ελλάδα ἕρχεται τό καλοκαίρι ἀπό τήν ᾿Αφρική. Φτιάχνει τή φωλιά του σέ ἀπόκρημνες ὄχθες, σέ κορμούς δένδρων κ.λ.π. ἀνοίγοντας μιά βαθιά τρύπα.

ROLLIER D'EUROPE: Grand oiseau, mesurant 30 cm., entre les plus beaux d'Europe. En été, il laisse l'Afrique pour la Grèce où il fait son nid en creusant un trou profond dans les falaises, dans les troncs des arbres etc.

BLAURACKE: Ein großer Vogel (30 cm), der zu den schösten Europas zählt. Nach Griechenland kommt er im Sommer von Afrika. Sein Nest baut er an steilen Küsten in Baumstämmen etc., indem er ein tiefes Loch aushöhlt.

GHIANDAIA: Grand'uccello di una lunghezza di circa 30 centimetri, uno dei più belli esistenti in Europa. In Grecia appare in estate, migrandovi dall'Africa. Nidifica lungo le rive, scegliendosi posti isolati, nei tronchi degli alberi ed altrove, aprendosi un passaggio profondo.

BLÅKRÅKA: En stor fågel, som är 30 cm lång, och en av de vackraste i Europa. Den kommer till Grekland på sommaren från Afrika. Den bygger boet vid branta stränder, i trädstammar etc. genom att göra ett djupt hål.

SCHARRELAAR: Een grote vogel van 30 cm. lengte, een van de mooiste vogels van Europa. 's Zomers trekt hij van Afrika naar Griekenland, waar hij zijn nest bouwt in steile oevers, in boomstammen e.d. door er een diep gat in te maken.

**16. Coracias
garrulus.**

ブッポウソウ

体長30cmの大きな鳥で、ヨーロッパで見られる鳥のうちでも最も美しいもののひとつ。
夏にアフリカからギリシャに渡ってくる。　海岸の崖、木の幹などに大きな穴を掘って巣を作る

BEE-EATER: One of the most beautiful of the Greek birds with stunningly coloured plumage. It arrives in Greece in the summer and makes its nest in steep cliff sides by excavating a hole. It inhabits high river banks and lake sides and, shallow-like, catches the insects it feeds on as it flies above the surface of the water. Length: 28 centimetres.

ΜΕΛΙΣΣΟΦΑΓΟΣ: ″Ενα από τά πιό όμορφα πουλιά μέ εκπληκτικά χρώματα. ″Ερχεται στήν ΄Ελλάδα τό καλοκαίρι καί φτιάχνει τή φωλιά του στίς απόκρημνες όχθες κάνοντας μιά τρύπα. Ζεῖ στίς όχθες τῶν ποταμῶν καί τῶν λιμνῶν καί πετάει σάν τό χελιδόνι πιάνοντας έντομα πάνω από τό νερό. Μῆκος 28 έκ.

GUEPIER D'EUROPE: Un des plus jolis oiseaux d'Europe, aux couleurs merveilleuses. Il vient en Grèce pour y passer l'été. Il creuse son trou dans les bords escarpés des lacs et des rivières. Comme l'hirondelle, il attrape au vol les insectes près de la surface de l'eau. Longueur: 28 cm.

BIENENFRESSER: Einer der schönsten griechischen Vögel mit überraschend schönen Farben. Er kommt im Sommer nach Griechenland und baut sein Nest in abschüssige Küsten, wo er ein Loch gräbt. Er lebt an den Ufern von Flüssen und Seen und fliegt wie die Schwalbe, indem er Insekten über dem Wasser fängt. Seine Länge ist 28 cm.

GRUCCIONE: Uno dei più begli uccelli viventi in Grecia dotato di un piumaggio a colori fantastici. Migra in Grecia in estate e nidifica lungo le rive in luoghi isolati, scavandosi un'apertura. Vive lungho le rive dei fiumi e dei laghi e vola come la rondine, beccando insetti sulla superficie delle acque. La sua lunghezza raggiunge 28 centimetri.

BIÄTARE: En av de vackraste fåglarna med underbara färger. Den kommer till Grekland på sommaren och bygger sitt bo i branta stränder genom att göra ett hål i stupet. Lever vid flod- och sjö-stränder, flyger som en svala och fångar insekter precis ovanför vattenytan. Längd 28 cm.

BIJENETER: Een der mooiste vogels, met schitterende kleuren. 's Zomers trekt hij naar Griekenland en bouwt hij daar zijn nest in steile oevers door het maken van een holte. Leeft aan rivier en meeroevers. Evenals de zwaluw vliegt hij, op jacht naar insecten, vlak boven het water. Lengte 28 cm.

**17. Merops
apiaster.**

ハチクイドリ

すばらしい色の羽毛を持ったギリシャでも最も美しい鳥の一種。 夏にギリシャに渡って
きて急な崖面に穴をあけて巣を作る。 川や湖の高い土手に棲息し、水面をかすめ
飛びながら、エサの昆虫を飲みこむようにして捕える。 体長28cm。

HOOPOE: A beautiful insectivore, 28 centimetres in length and characterised by its long-feathered crest which it can raise at will. It migrates from Africa to Greece in the summer, and creates its nest by digging a hole in a tree trunk.

ΤΣΑΛΑΠΕΤΕΙΝΟΣ: ᾿Ωραῖο πουλί μήκους 28 ἑκ. καί πολύ χαρακτηριστικό λοφίο ἀπό μεγάλα φτερά πού τά ὀρθώνει ὅποτε θέλει. ῎Ερχεται στήν ῾Ελλάδα ἀπό τήν ᾿Αφρική κάθε καλοκαίρι. Φτιάχνει τή φωλιά του σκάβοντας μιά τρύπα στόν κορμό ἑνός δένδρου. Τρέφεται μέ ἔντομα πού βρίσκει σκαλίζοντας τά σκουπίδια ἤ τήν κοπριά.

HUPPE FASCIEE: Bel oiseau, long de 28 cm., avec une huppe caractéristique faite de grandes plumes qu'il hausse à volonté. Il fait son nid en creusant un trou dans un tronc d'arbre. La huppe se nourrit d'insectes qu'elle trouve en fouillant dans les rebuts ou le fumier.

WIEDEHOPF: Ein schöner Vogel von 28 cm Länge mit einem sehr charakteristischen Schopf und großen Flügeln, die er - wenn er will - hebt. Nach Griechenland kommt er jeden Sommer von Afrika. Er baut sein Nest, indem er ein Loch in einen Baumstamm höhlt. Er nährt sich von Insekten, die er sich aus Abfall (Müll) oder Dung heraussucht.

UPUPA: Bell'uccello della lunghezza di 28 centimetri munito di una cresta guarnita di lunghe penne che innalza a volontà. Migra in Grecia, dall'Africa, ogni estate. Nidifica scavandosi un'apertura nei tronchi degli alberi. Si ciba d'insetti che scova nella spazzatura o nel letame.

HÄRFÅGEL: Vacker fågel, ungefär 28 cm lång, som har en mycket karakteristisk tofs av långa fjädrar, som den höjer när den vill. Den kommer varje sommar till Grekland från Afrika. Den bygger sitt bo genom att göra ett hål i en trädstam. Den äter insekter, som den finner i avfall och gödsel.

HOP: Een fraaie, 28 cm. lange vogel met een zeer kenmerkende kuif van grote veren, die hij naar believen rechtop kan zetten. Elke zomer komt hij uit Afrika naar Griekenland. Hij maakt zijn nest door een holte te maken in een boomstam. Zijn voedsel bestaat uit insecten, die hij in afval en mest vindt.

18. Upupa epops.

ヤツガシラ

体長28cmの美しい食虫鳥。　自在に建立てられる長い頭の毛が特徴。　夏にアフ
リカからギリシャに渡ってきて．木の幹に穴を堀って巣を作る。

GREAT SPOTTED WOODPECKER: An inhabitant of woodlands, where it feed on insects which it digs out of the bark or from rotting wood with its powerful beak. Its feet are four-clawed: two claws pointing forward and two back to give the bird better purchase on the vertical surface of the tree trunks. It is endemic to Northern Greece. Length: 22 centimetres. The red nape is only seen in the male.

ΠΑΡΔΑΛΟΤΣΙΚΛΙΤΑΡΑ: Ζεῖ στά δάση ὅπου τρέφεται μέ ἔντομα πού τά βρίσκει σκάβοντας τούς σάπιους κορμούς μέ τό δυνατό ράμφος του. Στά πόδια του τά δύο δάχτυλα εἶναι πρός τά ἐμπρός καί τά δύο πρός τά πίσω γιά νά στηρίζεται καλύτερα στό φλοιό τῶν δένδρων. Μῆκος 22 ἑκ. Ζεῖ στή Β. Ἑλλάδα ὅπου εἶναι ἐνδημικό.

PIC EPEICHE: Vit dans les forêts où il se nourrit d'insectes, de vers et de larves qu'il trouve en creusant les troncs pourris des arbres avec son bec puissant. Les doigts de ses pieds, bien separés, deux en avant et deux en arrière, lui permettent de se sentir plus surement perché sur les arbres. La tâche rouge existe seulement sur la tête des mâles.

BUNTSPECHT: Er lebt im Wald, wo er sich von Insekten nährt, die er mit seinem festen Schnabel aus morschen Baumstämmen ausgräbt. An seinen Füssen sehen zwei Zehen nach vorn und zwei nach hinten, so daß er sich besser an der Baumrinde festkrallen kann. Das weibliche Tier besitzt auf dem Kopf nicht die rote Zeichnung. Er lebt in Nordgriechenland als Zugvogel und seine Länge beträgt 22 cm.

PICCHIO ROSSO MAGGIORE: Vive nei boschi dove si ciba di insetti che riesce a trovare scavando nell'interno di tronchi marci, grazie al forte becco. Gli artigli anteriori e posteriori gli servono a poggiarsi meglio sulla scorza degli alberi. Raggiunge la lunghezza di 22 centimetri. Vive nella Grecia settentrionale in stato endemico.

STÖRRE HACKSPETT: Lever i skogar, där den äter insekter, som den finner i murkna stammar med sin kraftiga näbb. Två tår på foten är böjda framåt och två bakåt, för att den lättare skall kunna hålla sig fast vid barken på träden. 22 cm lång. Lever i norra Grekland, där den är inhemsk.

GROTE BONTE SPECHT: Leeft in bossen, waar hij zich voedt met insecten die hij bemachtigt door met zijn sterke snavel in vermolmde stammen te hakken. Zijn poten hebben twee voorwaarts en twee achterwaarts geplaatste tenen, zodat hij een beter houvast heeft aan de boombast. Alleen het mannetje heeft een rode vlek op de kop. Hij is inheems in Noord-Griekenland. Lengte 22 cm.

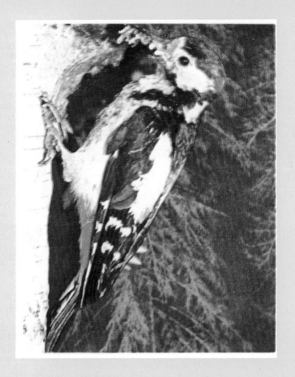

**19. Dendrocopus
major.**

オオマダラキツツキ

森林地帯に棲息し、強力なくちばしで朽ち木の樹皮をほって昆虫をつかまえる。
足には4つのツメがあり、2つは前に、2つは後に向いており、木の幹の垂直な面に止まり
やすいようになっている。　体長22cm．　北部ギリシャに特有．　うなじの赤い方がオ
スである。

GREEN WOODPECKER: A large bird, 32 centimetres in length, again with four-clawed feet for grasping the sides of tree trunks, where it pecks the bark to feed on the insects which nest there. It inhabits Northern Grrece all the year round, but is also found in the south during the winter. Only the male has the red cheek-markings illustrated here.

ΠΡΑΣΙΝΟΤΣΙΚΛΙΤΑΡΑ: Πουλί μεγάλο μήκους 32 έκ. Στά πόδια του τά δύο δάχτυλα εἶναι πρός τά ἐμπρός καί τά δύο πρός τά πίσω. Σκάβει τούς κορμούς τῶν σαπισμένων δένδρων καί τρώει τά ἔντομα πού φωλιάζουν ἐκεῖ. Ζεῖ ὅλον τόν χρόνο στή Β. ΄Ελλάδα. Τόν χειμώνα κατεβαίνει καί στά νότια μέρη τῆς χώρας.

PIC VERT: Grand oiseau,, long de 32 cm. Ses pieds ont quatre doigts, deux en avant et deux en arrière. Il creuse les troncs des arbres pourris et mange les insectes, les vers et les lavres qui y nichent. Il vit au nord de la Grèce pendant toute l'année. En hiver il descend au sud du pays.

GRUNSPECHT: Ein großer Vogel von 32 cm Länge. Zwei Zehen an seinen Füßen sehen nach vorne und zwei nach rückwärts. Er gräbt die Stämme morscher Bäume aus und frißt die Insekten, die dort nisten. Er kommt das ganze Jahr über in Nordgriechenland vor. Im Winter zieht er auch tiefer in den Süden des Landes.

PICCHIO VERDE: Uccello grande che raggiunge la lunghezza di 32 centimetri. Picchia i tronchi degli alberi marci col becco diritto e forte per farne uscire gli insetti dei quali si nutre. Vive per tutto l'anno nella Grecia settentrionale. Durante l'estate appare anche nelle regioni meridionali del paese.

GRÖNGÖLING: En stor fågel, på 32 cms längd. Två tår på foten är böjda framåt och två bakåt. Hackar i murkna trädstammar och äter insekter, som den finner där. Lever i norra Grekland under hela året. På vintern flyttar den även ner söderut i landet.

GROENE SPECHT: Een grote, 32 cm. lange vogel. De poten hebben twee voorwaarts en twee achterwaarts geplaatste tenen. Hij hakt in vermolmde boomstammen en eet de daarin nestelende insecten. Hij leeft het gehele jaar in Griekenland. 's Winters zakt hij ook af naar zuidelijker streken van het land.

20. Picus viridis.

ミドリキツツキ

体長32cmの大きな鳥で、木の幹に止まりやすいように4つのツメを持つ。 樹皮をつついて そこに住む昆虫を捕えてエサにする。 四季を通じて北部ギリシャに棲息するが、冬には南部にも見られる。 オスだけが頬に写真のような赤いもようを持つ。

CRESTED LARK: A very commonly found bird of 17 centimetres in length and characterised by its crest, this genus of lark lives in open plains and makes its nest in bushes. It is found throughout Greece and is non-migratory.

ΚΑΤΣΟΥΛΙΕΡΗΣ: Πολύ κοινό πουλί μήκους 17 έκ. καί χαρακτηριστικό λοφίο στό κεφάλι. Ζεῖ στίς ἀνοιχτές πεδιάδες καί κάνει τή φωλιά του στούς θάμνους. Ὑπάρχει σ᾽ ὁλόκληρη τήν Ἑλλάδα καί δέν μεταναστεύει.

CACHEVIS HUPPE: Oiseau très commun, long de 17 cm., avec une huppe caractéristique sur la tête. Il vit dans les plaines et fait son nid dans les buissons. Il se trouve dans toutes les régions de la Grèce où il vit pendant toute l'année.

HAUBENLERCHE: Ein sehr verbreiteter Vogel von 17 cm Länge und einem charakteristischen Schopf. Er lebt in den offenen Ebenen und nistet in den Büschen. Er kommt überall in Griechenland vor und wandert nicht aus.

CAPPELLACCIA: Uccello comunissimo della lunghezza di 17 centimetri, munito di una cresta caratteristica. Vive nelle pianure e nidifica tra i cespugli. Vive in tutta la Grecia e non migra.

TOFSLÄRKA: Mycket vanlig fågel, som är 17 cm lång, med en karakteristisk tofs på huvudet. Lever på öppna fält och bygger sitt bo i buskar. Man finner den över hela Grekland och den flyttar inte.

KUIFLEEUWERIK: Een zeer veel voorkomende vogel in Griekenland, met een kenmerkende kuif op de kop. Hij leeft op open terreinen en maakt zijn nest in struiken. Komt overal in Griekenland voor, en is geen trekvogel. Lengte 17 cm.

**21. Galerida
cristata.**

カンムリヒバリ

体長17cmの大へん良く見られる鳥で頭部に特徴がある。 ヒバリの種類。 広々
とした平野に住み, かん木の中に巣を作る。 ギリシャ全土に棲息する留鳥である。

SWALLOW: A very familiar bird of 19 centimetres in overall length. It comes to Greece in the Spring and nests under the overhangs of roofs or city balconies, or wherever it can find suitably protected niches. It feeds on insects it catches in flight.

ΣΤΑΥΡΟΧΕΛΙΔΟΝΟ: Πολύ γνωστό πουλί μήκους 19 έκ. ώς τήν ἄκρη τῆς οὐρᾶς. "Ερχεται τήν ἄνοιξη στήν 'Ελλάδα καί φτιάχνει τή φωλιά του στίς πόλεις κάτω ἀπό μπαλκόνια μέσα στίς βεράντες καί γενικά ὅπου ὑπάρχουν κατάλληλες προφυλαγμένες κόγχες. Τρέφεται μέ ἔντομα πού τά πιάνει πετώντας στόν ἀέρα.

HIRONDELLE DE CHEMINEE: Oiseau très connu, mesurant 19 cm. du bec jusqu'au bout de la queue, l'hirondelle vient en Grèce au printemps et fait son nid dans les villes, sous les balcons, sur les terraces et, en général, dans les coins ou elle peut se sentir bien a l'abri. Elle se nourrit d'insectes qu'elle attrape au vol.

RÖTELSCHWALBE: Ein sehr bekannter Vogel von 19 cm Länge bis zur Schwanzspitze. Er kommt im Frühling nach Griechenland und baut sein Nest in den Städten unter den Balkonen, in den Veranden und allgemein überall dort wo es geschützte geeignete Mauernischen gibt. Er nährt sich von Insekten, die er im Fluge fängt.

RONDINE: Uccello notissimo della lunghezza di 19 centimetri fino all'estremità della codina. Migra in Grecia durante l'estate e nidifica nelle città sotto i balconi, nelle terrazze ed in genere nei luoghi in cui si sente preservata. Si ciba di insetti che becca mentre vola.

SVALA: Mycket känd fågel, som är 19 cm lång ända ut till stjärtspetsen. Den kommer till Grekland på våren och bygger sitt bo i ett passande och skyddat hörn under balkongerna, vid verandor, i städerna och byar. Den jagar insekter i luften till föda.

BOERENZWALUW: Een 19 cm. lange, zeer bekende vogel, die in de lente naar Griekenland trekt en zijn nest bouwt op de steden onder balkons, in veranda's en in het algemeen overal waar een geschikt beschut hoekje is. hij voedt zich met insecten die hij in de vlucht vangt.

**22. Hirundo
rustica.**

ツバメ

体長19cmの大へんなじみ深い鳥。　春にギリシャに渡ってきて、屋根や町のバルコニーの張出しの下など、どこにでもちょうどよいかくれ家を見つけて巣を作る。飛行中につかまえた昆虫をエサとする。

HOUSE MARTIN: The most familiar of the urban swallows, measuring only 12. centimetres. Like all members of the swallow family, it makes its nest of small globules of damp earth in suitably protected corners on buildings. It feeds on insects, which it hunts and catches on the wing. The house martin migrates to Africa for the winter.

ΣΠΙΤΟΧΕΛΙΔΟΝΟ: Τό πιό κοινό χελιδόνι τῶν πόλεων μήκους 12,5 ἑκ. Φτιάχνει τή φωλιά του στά σπίτια σέ κατάλληλες καί προφυλαγμένες θέσεις. Τρέφεται κυνηγώντας ἔντομα στόν ἀέρα. Τόν χειμώνα φεύγει γιά τήν ᾽Αφρική.

HIRONDELLE DE FENETRE: L'hirondelle de ville plus commune, mesurant 12,5 cm. Elle construit son nid sous les toits des maisons où elle peut se sentir a l'abri. Elle se nourrit d'insectes qu'elle attrape au vol. Quand vient l'hiver, l'hirondelle émigre en Afrique.

HAUSSCHWALBE: Die in den Städten am meisten vorkommende Schwalbenart. Diese Schwalbe ist 12,5 cm lang und baut sein Nest in Häusern, und zwar in geeigneten und geschützen Stellen. Sie nährt sich von Insekten, die sie im Fluge fängt. Im Winter zieht sie nach Afrika.

RONDONE: La rondine più comune delle città. Raggiunge la lunghezza di 12 centimetri. Nidfica nella case in posti adatti e ben preservati. Si ciba d'insetti che acchiappa al suolo. Durante l'inverno migra in Africa.

HUSSVALA: Den vanligaste svalan i städerna med en längd av 12,5 cm. Även den bygger sitt bo vid husens mest skyddade och passande platser. Den föder sig genom att jaga insekter i luften. På vintern flyttar den till Afrika.

23. Delichon
urbica.

イワツバメ

都市のツバメの中では最もおなじみのもので, 体長I2.5cm. 他のツバメ族と同
様, 建物ののきさしに, 泥で小さな丸い巣を作る. 飛行中つかまえた昆虫をエサと
する. 冬にアフリカから渡ってくる.

GOLDEN ORIOLE: *An outstandingly beautiful bird, 24 centimetres in length. The female has olive-coloured plumage along the back and is grey-white with darker markings on the underside. The golden oriole migrates from Africa in the summer and nests in the woods of northern-most Central Greece.*

ΣΥΚΟΦΑΓΟΣ: *῾Ωραῖο πουλί μήκους 24 ἑκ. Τό θηλυκό ἔχει χρῶμα λαδί ἀπό πάνω καί γκριζόλευκο μέ σκοῦρα στίγματα στήν κοιλιά. ῎Ερχεται.τό καλοκαίρι ἀπό τήν ᾽Αφρική καί φωλιάζει μέσα στά δάση, βορειότερα ἀπό τήν Κεντρική ῾Ελλάδα.*

LORIOT JAUNE: *Joli oiseau, mesurant 24 cm. La femelle a le dos vert bouteille et le ventre gris-blanc tâché de noir. Le loriot vient d'Afrique pour passer l'été en Grèce où il fait son nid dans les forêts, de préférance celles du centre-nord.*

PIROL: *Ein schöner Vogel mit einer Länge von 24 cm. Das weibliche Tier besitzt auf dem Rücken eine dunkelgrüne Farbe und ist auf dem Bauch grauweiß mit dunklen Zeichnungen. Der Pirol kommt im Sommer auf Afrika und nistet in den Wäldern, und zwar nördlich von Zentralgriechenland.*

BECCAFICO: *Bell'uccello della lunghezza di 24 centimetri. La femmina ha il piumaggio di color verde oliva nella parte superiore e il ventre grigio-bianco tempestato di macchie scure. Migra in estate dall'Africa e nidifica nei boschi sparsi a nord della Grecia centrale.*

SOMMARGYLLING: *En vacker, ungefär 24 cm lång fågel. Honan har olivgrön färg på översidan, och gråvit med mörka fläckar på magen. Den kommer hit på sommaren från Afrika och bygger bo i skogen, norr om Mellan-Grekland.*

WIELEWAAL: *Een mooie vogel. Zijn Griekse naam betekent letterlijk "vijgeneter". Het wijfje is van boven olijfgroen, en van onder grijswit met donkere vlekken. hij komt in de zomer uit Afrika, en nestelt in de bossen ten Noorden van Centraal-Griekenland. Lengte 24 cm.*

**24. Oriolus
oriolus.**

コウライウグイス

体長24cmの大へん美しい鳥。 メスは、背はオリーブ色、腹はこいもようを浮かべた白灰色の羽毛を持つ。 夏にアフリカから渡ってきて、中部ギリシャの北部の森林に巣を作る。

MAGPIE: This is a bird found in great numbers throughout Greece, and is about 45 centimetres in length. It is omnivorous, and a permanent non-migratory resident.

ΚΑΡΑΚΑΞΑ: Πολύ κοινό πουλί σ' όλόκληρη τήν Ἑλλάδα. Ἔχει μῆκος γύρω στά 45 έκ. Εἶναι πουλί παμφάγο καί δέν μεταναστεύει τό χειμώνα.

PIC: Oiseau très connu dans toute la Grèce. Il mesure environ 45 cm. Il mange de tout et n'émigre pas en hiver.

ELSTER: Ein in ganz Griechenland weitverbreiteter Vogel. Er ist rd. 45 cm lang. Er ist ein Allesfresser und verzieht im Winter nicht.

GAZZA: Uccello comunissimo in tutta la Grecia. Raggiunge la lunghezza di circa 45 centimetri. Si nutre di tutto e non migra durante l'inverno.

SKATA: En mycket vanlig fågel i hela Grekland. Den är omkring 45 cm lång. Den äter allt och flyttar inte på vintern.

EKSTER: Een overal in Griekenland veel voorkomende vogel. Lengte ongeveer 45 cm. Een alles-eter. hij trekt in de winter niet weg naar elders.

25. Pica pica.

カササギ

ギリシャに多数棲息する鳥で、体長約45cm。 何でもエサとする留鳥である。

DIPPER: An inhabitant of the steep banks of mountain streams, the dipper feeds on a variety of acquatic insects and other water creatures. To catch them, it dives right down into the icy water and walks along the rocky bottom. The yound are plain grey in colour. Length 18-20 centimetres.

ΝΕΡΟΚΟΤΣΥΦΑΣ: Τό πουλί αὐτό ζεῖ στίς ὄχθες τῶν ὀρεινῶν ποταμῶν. ῾Η τροφή του ἀποτελεῖται ἀπό διάφορα ὑδρόβια ἔντομα κι ἄλλα μικρά ζῶα τοῦ νεροῦ. Γιά νά πιάσει βουτάει στά παγωμένα νερά καί περπατάει στόν βραχώδη βυθό Τό θηλυκό ἔχει ὁμοιόμορφο σταχτί χρῶμα. Μῆκος 18-20 ἑκ.

CINCCLE PLONGEUR: Cet oiseau vit sur les rives des fleuves aux régions montagneuses. Il se nourrit d'insectes aquatiques et autres petits animaux qui vivent dans les rivières. Il les attrape en plongeant dans l'eau glacée et marche sur le lit rocailleux du fleuve. La femelle a le plumage gris uni. Longueur: 18-20 cm.

WASSERAMSEL: Dieser Vogel lebt an den Ufern der Gebirgsflüsse. Seine Nahrung besteht aus verschiedenen wasserlebenden Insekten und anderen kleinen Wassergetier. Um sie zu fangen, taucht er ins eiskalte Wasser und schreitet auf dem felsigen Grund. Das weibliche Tier besitzt eine gleichmäßige graue Färbung. Seine Länge beträgt 18-20 cm.

MERLO ACQUATICO: Quest'uccello vive lungo le rive dei fiumi in regioni montagnose. Si ciba di vari insetti ed altri animaletti acquatici. Per pescarli si tuffa nelle acque gelide e cammina sul fondo roccioso. La femmina ha il piumaggio di colore cenere uniforme. Raggiunge la lunghezza di 18-20 centimetri.

STRÖMSTARE: Denna fågel lever vid bergsflodernas stränder. Dess föda består av olika vatteninsekter och andra små vattendjur. För att fånga dem, dyker den ner i det iskalla vattnet och går på klippbotten. Honan har jämn grå färg. Längden på strömstaren är ungefär 18-20 cm.

WATERSPREEUW: Deze vogel leeft aan de oevers van bergstromen. Zijn voedsel bestaat uit verschillende soorten waterinsecten en andere kleine waterdieren. Om die te vangen duikt hij in het ijskoude water en loopt op de rotsachtige rivierbedding. Het wijfje is egaal grijs. Lengte 18-20 cm.

**26. Cinclus
cinclus.**

カワガラス

山の川の急な土手に棲息し. 体長18～20cm.　冷たい水に飛びこみ、川底の岩
の上を歩いて. 水に住む種々の昆虫や動物をつかまえてエサとする.　若鳥は地味
な灰色をしている.

BLACK REDSTART: A common bird in Greece, where it lives all the year round. Both female and male are grey all over except for the tail which is brown. The black redstart, an insectivore, summers in the mountains, but migrates to lower-lying fields, shorelines and cities in winter. Length: 14 centimetres.

ΚΑΡΒΟΥΝΙΑΡΗΣ: Πουλί ἀρκετά κοινό στήν ʹΕλλάδα ὅπου μένει ὅλον τόν χρόνο. Τό θηλυκό ἔχει ὁμοιόμορφο γκρίζο χρῶμα ἐκτός ἀπό τήν οὐρά πού εἶναι καφέ ὅπως τοῦ ἀρσενικοῦ. ʹΟ Καρβουνιάρης τρέφεται μέ ἔντομα. Τό καλοκαίρι ἀνεβαίνει στά βουνά ἐνῶ τό χειμώνα ἔρχεται στούς κάμπους, στίς ἀκτές καί στίς πόλεις.

ROUGE-QUEUE NOIR: Oiseau assez commun en Grèce, où il vit pendant toute l'année. La femelle a le plumage gris uni et la queue marron comme celle du mâle. Le rougequeue se nourrit d'insectes. Pendant l'été il vole vers les montagnes tandis qu'en hiver il descend dans les vallées, les rivages et les villes.

HAUSROTSCHWANZ: Ein in Griechenland ziemlich häufig vorkommender Vogel, der hier das ganze Jahr über anzutreffen ist. Das weibliche Tier ist von gleichmäßig grauer Farbe mit Ausnahme des Schwanzes, der braun gefärbt ist, wie übrigens auch das männliche Tier. Der Hausrotschwanz nährt sich von Insekten. Im Sommer zieht er in die Berge, während er im Winter in die Ebenen, Küsten und Städte niedersteigt.

CODIROSSO: Uccello assai comune in Grecia ove vive per tutto l'inverno. La femmina ha il piumaggio coperto di colore grigio, tranne la coda, simile a quella del maschio, di color marrone. Si ciba di insetti. Durante l'estate sale sulle montagne mentre nella stagione invernale scende nei campi o lo si trova lungo le rive e nelle città.

SVART RÖDSTJÄRT: En ganska vanlig fågel i Grekland, där den lever hela året om. Honan har en jämn grå färg utom på stjärten, som är brun såsom hanens. Den svarta rödstjärten äter insekter. På sommaren flyttar den upp i bergen, medan den på vintern kommer ner på fälten, till kusterna och städerna.

ZWARTE ROODSTAART: Een in Griekenland vrij veel voorkomende vogel, die er het gehele jaar blijft. Het wijfje is egaal grijs, afgezien van de staart die bruin is, evenals die van het mannetje. Het voedsel bestaat uit insecten. 's Zomers zoekt hij de bergen op, terwijl hij 's winters naar de dalen, kuststreken en steden trekt.

27. Phoenicurus ochruros.

クロジョウビタキ

四季を通じてギリシャに一般に見られる鳥で昆虫をエサとする。　オス・メスとも灰色
で尾だけが茶色をしている。　夏には山に住むが、冬になると低地の平野や海岸、
町に移る。　体長14cm。

ROBIN: This is a very familiar, non-migratory bird in Greece. It constructs its nest under bushes, in scrub land or in open wooded areas. The young are a speckled grey-chestnut in colour with markings in lighter shades. Length: 14 centimetres.

ΚΟΚΚΙΝΟΛΑΙΜΗΣ: Πολύ γνωστό στήν 'Ελλάδα πουλί. Δέν μεταναστεύει. Κατασκευάζει τή φωλιά του κάτω άπό θάμνους. Ζεῖ σέ θαμνότοπους καί μέρη μέ άραιά δάση. Τό θηλυκό εἶναι όμοιόχρωμο καστανο-σταχτί μέ πιό άνοιχτόχρωμα στίγματα.

ROUGE-GORGE: Oiseau non-migrateur très connu en Grèce. Il construit son nid sous les buissons. Il vit dans le maquis et les régions peu boisées. Le plumage de la femelle est gris-marron avec des tâches plus claires.

ROTKEHLCHEN: Ein in Griechenland sehr bekannter Vogel. Er wandert nicht aus. Sein Nest baut er unter Büschen. Er lebt im Gebüsch und in lichten Wäïc©ldern. Das weibliche Tier hat eine einheitlich grau-Kastanienbraune Färbung mit hellfarbigeren Punkten.

PETTIROSSO: Notissimo in Greica. Non migra. Nidifica tra i cespugli. Vive in zone cespugliose o in boschi radi. La femmina è coperta di un piumaggio di colore cenere uniforme picchiettato di macchie più chiare.

RÖDHAKE: Mycket välkänd fågel i Grekland. Den flyttar inte. Bygger sitt bo under buskar. Den lever i buskvegetation och platser med gles skog. Honan är jämnt gråbrun med fläckar i ljusare färg.

ROODBORST: Een in Griekenland zeer bekende vogel. Hij bouwt zijn nest onder struikgewas, en leeft op met struikgewas begroeide plaatsen en in open bossen. Het wijfje is egaal grijsbruin met lichtere plekken. De roodborst trekt niet weg uit Griekenland.

**28. Erithacus
rubecula.**

コマドリ

ギリシャでは大へんなじみ深い鳥で留鳥、 かん木地帯や、広々とした森林地帯
の低い木の下に巣を作る。 若鳥は明るいもようを浮かべたまだらの茶灰色をしている。
体長14cm.

NIGHTINGALE: Every Greek recognises the nightingale by its song. Very few are aware, however, that those lovely melodies are produced by a bird so dull in colour. The nightingale is a summer visitor to Greece. It is 16 centimetres in length and feeds on insects.

ΑΗΔΟΝΙ: Στήν ΄Ελλάδα ὅλοι γνωρίζουν τό ἀηδόνι ἀπό τό κελάϊδημά του. Οἱ περισσότεροι ὅμως δέν φαντάζονταν ὅτι οἱ θαυμάσιες μελωδίες, πού ἀκούγονται τήν νύχτα στίς δροσερές ρεματιές, προέρχονται ἀπό ἕνα πουλί μέ τόσο κοινά χρώματα. Τό ἀηδόνι ἔρχεται στήν ΄Ελλάδα τό καλοκαίρι. ῎Εχει μῆκος 16 ἑκ. Τρέφεται μέ ἔντομα.

ROSSIGNOL PHILOMELE: En Grèce tout le monde conna''t le chant du rossignol. La plupart, cependant, ne s'imaginent pas que les mélodies merveilleuses que l'on entend la nuit aux proximités des ravins, proviennent d'un oiseau aux couleurs si communes. Le rossignol vient en Grèce pour l'été. Il mesure 16 cm. et se nourrit d'insectes.

NACHTIGALL: Alle kennen die Nachtigall von ihrem Gesang her. Die meisten jedoch wissen nicht, daß die wunderbaren Melodien, die sie in her Nacht in kühlen Schluchten vernehmen, von einem Vogel mit so gewöhnlichem Federkleid stammen. Die Nachtigall kommt im Sommer nach Griechenland. Die Nachtigall nährt sich von Insekten und besitzt eine Länge von 16 cm.

USIGNOLO: Uccello molto pregiato in Grecia per la dolcezza del suo canto. La maggior parte dei suoi ammiratori forse non si immaginano che le dolci melodie che ascoltano con tanta delizia provengono da un uccello coperto di un piumaggio i cui colori sono di un ordinario esasperante. L'usignolo migra in Grecia in estate. Ha una lunghezza di circa sedici centimetri. Si ciba di insetti.

NÄKTERGAL: I Grekland känner alla igen näktergalens melodiska sång. De flesta föreställer sig dock ej att dess underbara toner, som man hör på natten vid de svala flodbäddarna, kommer från en fågel med så vanliga och enkla färger. Näktergalen flyttar till Grekland på sommaren. Den är 16 cm lång och livnär sig på insekter.

NACHTEGAAL: In Griekenland kent iedereen de nachtegaal door zijn gezang. De meeste mensen hebben er echter geen idee van dat de wondermooie melodiën, die 's nachts te beluisteren zijn in koele dalen, afkomstig zijn van een zo gewoon gekleurde vogel. De nachtegaal komt 's zomers naar Griekenland. Hij voedt zich met insecten. Lengte 16 cm.

29. Luscinia
megarhynchos.

ヨナキウグイス

ギリシャ人なら誰でもこの鳥の歌声を知っているが、その美しい歌を歌っているのがどんなに目立たない色をした鳥であるかを知る者は少ない。　夏にギリシャに訪れる。
体長16cmで昆虫をエサとする。

SONG THRUSH: This bird is endemic to the forests of Northern Greece, but in harsh winters it often migrates to the South and to the islands. It is about 22 centimetres in length and feeds on insects and snails, which it extracts from their brittle shells by pounding them on a flat stone with its beak.

ΚΕΛΑΙΔΟΤΣΙΧΛΑ: Πουλί ἐνδημικό στά δάση τῆς Βόρειας Ἑλλάδας. Στήν βαρυχειμωνιά κατεβαίνει συχνά στά νότια μέρη καί στά νησιά. Τό μῆκος του εἶναι γύρω στά 22 ἑκ. Τρέφεται μέ ἔντομα καί σαλιγκάρια.

GRIVE MUSICIENNE: Elle vit habituellement dans les bois du nord de la Grèce mais, quand l'hiver est très rigide, elle descend vers le sud et les "les. Elle mesure 22 cm. environ et se nourrit d'insectes et d'escargots.

SINGDROSSEL: Ein in den Wäldern Nordgriechenlands als Zugvogel lebender Vogel. Im tiefen Winter kommt er häufig nach Süden und auf die Inseln herunter. Seine Länge ist rd. 22 cm. er nährt sich von Insekten und Schnecken.

TORDO: Uccello endemico delle foreste della Grecia settentrionale. Durante la stagione invernale, nei giorni più freddi, scende verso le regioni più meridionali e nelle isole. La sua lunghezza raggiunge circa i 22 centimetri. Si ciba di insetti e di lumache.

SÅNGTRAST: En vanligen inhemsk fågel, som lever i skogarna i Norra Grekland. Men under den kyligaste delen av vintern, flyttar den ofta ner till sydligare delar och till öarna. Den är omkring 22 cm lång. Den lever på insekter och sniglar.

ZANGLIJSTER: Een in de bossen van Noord-Griekenland inheemse vogel. In strenge winters trekt hij vaak naar zuidelijker streken en naar de eilanden. Hij voedt zich met insecten en slakken. Lengte ongeveer 22 cm.

30. Turdus philomelus.

ウタツグミ

北部ギリシャの森に特有の鳥であるが、寒い冬には しばしば 南部ギリシャや島に移っ
てくる。 体長約22cmで、昆虫と、くちばしで 平らな石の上に追いこんで カラをこわ
して中味をひっぱり出した カタツムリをエサとする。

GREAT TIT: This charming little bird, 14 centimetres in length, lives in the woods and feeds on caterpillars and insects. It does not migrate to other countries, but moves up to the mountains in summer and returns to lower altitudes in winter to take up residence in city parks and gardens.

ΚΑΛΟΓΕΡΟΣ: Τό χαριτωμένο αὐτό πουλί πού ἔχει μῆκος 14 ἑκ. ζεῖ στά δάση καί τρέφεται μέ κάμπιες καί ἔντομα. Δέν μεταναστεύει σ' ἄλλες χῶρες ἀλλά τό καλοκαίρι ἀνεβαίνει στά βουνά καί τόν χειμῶνα γυρίζει στά χαμηλά μέρη, στούς κήπους καί στά πάρκα τῶν πόλεων.

MESANGE CHARBONNIERE: Cet oiseau charmant qui mesure 14 cm., vit dans les forêts et se nourrit de chenilles et d'insectes. La mésange n'emigre pas mais, pendant l'été, vole vers les montagnes tandis qu'en hiver elle préfère les régions plus basses, et même les jardins et les parcs publics.

KOHLMEISE: Dieser liebenswürdige Vogel, der 14 cm lang ist, lebt in den Wäldern und n³/₄hrt sich von Raupen und Insekten. Er zieht nicht in andere Länder, aber im Sommer zieht er in die Berge und im Winter kehrt er in die tiefergelegenen Gegenden zurück, in die Gärten und Parks der Städte.

CINCIALLEGRA: Questo grazioso uccello che vive nei boschi e la cui lunghezza raggiunge i 14 centimetri si ciba di insetti e di bachi. Non migra in altri paesi, però durante l'estate sale verso zone montuose per ridiscendere in inverno in regioni più basse, nei giardini e nei parchi pubblici.

Denna förtjusande lilla fågel, som är 14 cm lång, lever i skogarna och föder sig på maskar och insekter. Den flyttar inte till andra länder, men flyger under sommaren upp i bergen, medan den under vintern föredrar trädgårdar och stadsparker i trakter på lägre höjd.

KOOLMEES: Deze aardige, 14 cm. lange vogel leeft in bossen en voedt zich met larven en insecten. Hij trekt niet weg naar andere landen, maar 's zomers gaat hij de bergen in en 's winters keert hij terug naar lagere streken, naar tuinen en stadsparken.

31. Parus major.

オオヤマガラ

体長14cmのこの愛らしい鳥は林に棲息し、蝶や蛾の幼虫や虫をエサとする。
外国には渡らないが、夏には山に上ってきて、冬になると又町の公園や庭などの低地
に戻っていく。

NUTHATCH: This is a common bird in all the woods and forests of Greece, wintering at low altitudes and spending the summers in the mountains. It feeds on insects, which it finds in the fissures of tree trunks as well as on acorns and pinecone and other seeds. It makes its nest by hollowing out the rotten trunk of some dead tree, leaving only a tiny aperture as an entrance. *Length: 14 centimetres.*

ΔΕΝΔΡΟΤΣΟΠΑΝΑΚΟΣ: Πουλί κοινό στά δάση ὅλης τῆς Ἑλλάδας. Τόν χειμώνα κατεβαίνει στά χαμηλά μέρη ἐνῶ τό καλοκαίρι πηγαίνει στά βουνά. Τρέφεται μέ ἔντομα πού βρίσκει ψάχνοντας στίς σχισμές τοῦ κορμοῦ τῶν δένδρων καθώς καί μέ βελανίδια κι ἄλλους σπόρους. Τή φωλιά του τήν σκάβει στό σάπιο κορμό κάποιου ξεροῦ δένδρου. Χτίζει τήν εἴσοδο ἀφήνοντας μιά μικρή τρύπα.

SITTELLE TORCHEPOT: Oiseau mesurant 14 cm., commun aux forêts de toute la Grèce. En hiver, il fréquente les régions basses tandis qu'en été il monte vers les montagnes. Il se nourrit d'insectes (qu'il découvre dans les craquelures de l'écorce des arbres) ainsi que de glandes et autres graines. Il creuse son nid dans le tronc pourri des arbres desséchés. Il mure l'entrée en laissant un petit trou pour ses allées et venues.

KLEIBER: Ein in den Wäldern Griechenlands häufig anzutreffender Vogel. Im Winter kommt er in die tiefergelegenen Gebiete herunter, während er im Sommer in die Berge hinaufzieht. Er nährt sich von Insekten, die er sich aus den Rissen der Baumstämme heraussucht sowie auch von Eicheln und anderen Samen. Sein Nestbaut er in den morschen Stamm eines trockenen Baumes. Er baut den Eingang, indem er eine kleine Offnung freiläßt.

SITTA EUROPEA: Uccello comunissimo che s'incontra nei boschi di tutta la Grecia. Raggiunge la lunghezza di 14 centimetri. Durante l'inverno vive in regioni basse, mentre d'estate sale nelle zone montuose. Si ciba d'insetti che scova nelle fessure dei tronchi, nonché di ghiande e di altri semi. Nidifica nel tronco marcio degli alberi insecchiti. Si costruisce l'ingresso del nido lasciandovi una piccola apertura.

NÖTVÄCKA: En vanlig fågel i skogarna över hela Grekland. På vintern flyttar den ner på låg höjd, medan den på sommaren flyttar upp i bergen. Födan består av insekter, som den söker i barkspringor i trädstammar, och ekollon och andra frön. Den gräver i en murken stam på något dött träd för att bygga sitt bo. Den murar igen öppningen och lämnar bara ett litet hål öppet.

BOOMKLEVER: Een in de bossen van heel Griekenland veel voorkomende vogel. In de winter trekt hij naar laaggelegen streken, in de zomer naar de bergen. Hij voedt zich met insecten, die hij in spleten in boomstammen vindt, en met eikels en andere zaden. Zijn nest boort hij uit in de vermolmde stam van een dorre boom. Als ingang laat hij een klein gaatje open.

**32. Sitta
europea.**

ゴジュウカラ

ギリシャ全土の森林地帯に住む一般的な鳥で、冬には低地に夏には山に棲息する。
木の幹の裂け目にいる昆虫やしいの実、松の実などの実をエサとする。　枯れた木の朽ち
た幹に小さな入口を残した穴をほって巣を作る。

CHAFFINCH: A very common species found in mountain forests in the summer and in lower-lying plains in winter. It feeds on seeds, and constructs twiggy nests in trees. Length: 15 centimetres. Shown here is a male in winter plumage. The female is yellowish-brown above, shading into a lighter grey below.

ΣΠΙΝΟΣ: Πολύ κοινό εἶδος πού τό καλοκαίρι ζεῖ στά δάση τῶν βουνῶν καί τόν χειμώνα κατεβαίνει στίς πεδιάδες. Τρέφεται μέ σπόρους. Τή φωλιά του τή χτίζει πάνω στά δένδρα.

PINSON DES ARBRES: Espèce très commune qui, en été, vit dans les forêts des montagnes et, en hiver, descend dans les vallées et les plaines. Le pinson se nourrit de graines et fait son nid sur les arbres. Longueur: 15 cm.

BUCHFINK: Eine sehr verbreitete Vogelart, die im Sommer in den Bergwäldern lebt und im Winter in die Ebenen herunterzieht. Der Buchfink nährt sich von Samen. Sein Nest baut er oben auf Bäumen.

FRINGUELLO: Uccello comunissimo di una lunghezza di 15 cm. che durante l'estate vive nei boschi montuosi mentre nei mesi invernali cerca rifugio nelle pianure. Si ciba di semi. Nidifica sugli alberi.

BOFINK: Mycket vanlig fågel, som på sommaren lever i skogarna i bergen och på vintern flyttar ner till lågslätterna. Den äter frön. Sitt bo bygger den högt uppe i träden.

VINK: Een zeer veel voorkomende vogelsoort, die 's zomers in de bergwouden en 's winters in lager gelegen gebieden verblijft. Hij voedt zich met zaden. Zijn nest bouwt hij boven in bomen. Lengte 15 cm.

33. Fringilla
coelebs.

アトリ

夏には山の森に、冬には低地の平野に見られる大へん一般的な鳥。　植物の種をエサ
とし、木の中に小枝を集めて巣を作る。　体長15cm。　写真は冬のオスの姿で、メスは
背は黄色がかった茶色で、腹にかけて明るい灰色になっている。

GOLDFINCH: A well-known species in Greece, the goldfinch lives in open scrub land where it feeds on all kinds of seeds. In summer it moves up to the cooler mountains, but in winter it can be found living in the plains. Length: 12 centimetres.

ΚΑΡΔΕΡΙΝΑ: Είδος πολύ γνωστό στήν Ἑλλάδα. Ζεῖ στούς ἀνοιχτούς θαμνότοπους ὅπου τρέφεται μέ διάφορους σπόρους. Τό καλοκαίρι ἀνεβαίνει στά δροσερά βουνά ἐνῶ τόν χειμώνα τό βρίσκουμε στούς κάμπους.

CHARDONNET: Espèce très connue en Grèce. Il vit dans les maquis où il trouve les graines dont il se nourrit. En été il recherche la fra"cheur des montagnes tandis qu'en hiver nous le trouvons dans les plaines. Longueur: 12 cm.

STIEGLITZ: In Griechenland sehr bekannt. Der Stieglitz lebt an offenen mit Büschen bestandenen Plätzen, wo er sich von Samen nährt. Im Sommer zieht er in die kühlen Bierge, während er den Winter auf den Feldern verbringt.

CARDELLINO: Uccello notissimo in Grecia. Vive in zone cespugliose. Si ciba di vari semi. Durante i mesi estivi sale in zone montuose, mentre d'inverno lo troviamo nei campi. Ha una lunghezza di circa dodici centimetri.

STEGLITS: Mycket känd fågel i Grekland. Den lever på öppna buskmarker, där den äter olika frön. På sommaren flyttar den upp i de svala bergen, medan man på vintern finner den nere på slätterna.

PUTTER: Een zeer bekende vogelsoort in Griekenland, die op schaars begroeide plaatsen leeft, waar hij zich voedt met allerlei zaden. 's Zomers zoekt hij het hogerop in de koele bergen, terwijl wij hem's winters in de vlakten vinden. Lengte 12 cm.

**34. Carduelis
carduelis.**

ヒワ

ギリシャではよく知られた鳥で、広々とした かん木地帯に棲息し、様々の種子をエサと
する。 冬には平野に住むが、夏には涼しい山に移ってくる。 体長12cm.

LINNET: A bird found throughout Greece, in scrub land, as well as in city gardens and parks. It is a herbivore, living strictly on seeds. Length: 13 centimetres. During the mating season the male is resplendent in a red crown and breast.

ΚΟΚΚΙΝΟΣΠΙΖΑ: Πουλί κοινό σ' ὁλόκληρη τήν Ἑλλάδα. Ζεῖ στούς θαμνότοπους, στούς κήπους καί στά πάρκα ψάχνοντας γιά διάφορους σπόρους πού ἀποτελοῦν τήν τροφή του. Μῆκος 13 ἑκ.

LINOTTE MELODIEUSE: Oiseau très commun dans toute la Grèce. Il vit dans le maquis, les parcs et les jardins publics où il trouve les graines nécessaires à sa nourriture. Longueur: 13 cm.

HÄNFLIGN: Ein in Griechenland verbreiteter Vogel von 13 cm Länge. Er lebt im Gebüsch, in Gärten und in Parks, wo er nach verschiedenen Samen sucht, die seine Nahrung bilden.

FANELLO: Uccello comunissimo che s'incontra in tutta la Grecia. Vive nelle zone cespugliose, nei giardini e nei parchi pubblici cercando di cibarsi di vari semi. La sua lunghezza raggiunge i 13 centimetri.

HÄMPLING: En vanlig fågel över hela Grekland. Den häckar i buskvegetation, i trädgårdar, och i parker och söker efter olika frön, som dess föda består av.

KNEU: Een overal in Griekenland voorkomende vogel, die op met struikgewas begroeide plaatsen, in tuinen en in plantsoenen leeft, waar hij naar allerlei zaden zoekt die zijn voedsel vormen. In de paartijd is het mannetje getooid met een rood voorhoofd en een rode borst. Lengte 13 cm.

**35. Acanthis
cannabina.**

ベニヒワ

かん木地帯、町の庭、公園などギリシャ全域で見られる鳥。　種子のみをエサにする草食鳥。　体長13cm。　オスは交尾期には赤いトサカと脳がキラキラ輝くようになる。

CROSSBILL: A mountain bird which very rarely descends to lower altitudes. It feeds on the seeds of the different varieties of pine and fir trees of the great forests of the mountainous Greek North. In Spring the male takes on a deep red hue, while the plumage of the female becomes greenish in colour. The crossbill nests in trees. Length: 16 centimetres.

ΕΛΑΤΟΣΤΑΥΡΟΜΥΤΗΣ: Πουλί τῶν βουνῶν πού σπάνια κατεβαίνει στά χαμηλά μέρη. Τρέφεται μέ τούς σπόρους ἀπό διάφορα εἴδη πεύκων καί ἐλάτων πού σχηματίζουν μεγάλα δάση στά ἑλληνικά βουνά. Τήν ἄνοιξη τό ἀρσενικό παίρνει ἔντονο κόκκινο χρῶμα ἐνῶ τό θηλυκό γίνεται πρασινωπό. Κάνουν τή φωλιά τους στά δένδρα. Μῆκος 16 ἑκ.

BEC-CROISE DES SAPINS: Oiseau des montagnes, qui descend rarement dans les régios basses. Il se nourrit de toutes sortes de graines des pins et des sapins des grandes forêts sur les montagnes. Au printemps le mâle prend une vive couleur rouge tandis que le plumage de la femelle vire au vert. Ils construisent leur nid sur les arbres. Longueur: 16 cm.

FICHTENKREUZSCHNABEL: Ein Gebirgsvogel, der selten in niedrig gelegene Gegenden zieht. Er nährt sich von Samen verschiedener Fichten und Tannenbäume, die große Wälder in den griechischen Bergen bilden. Im Frühling nimmt das männliche Tier eine starke rötliche Färbung an, während das weibliche Tier sein Federkleid ins Grünliche färbt. Dieser Vogel nistet hoch in den Bäumen. er wird 16 cm lang.

CROCIERE: Uccello delle montagne, che raramente discende nelle regioni basse. Si ciba di ogni sorta di semi dei pini e degli abeti delle foreste sparse su per i monti della Grecia. In primavera il maschio prende un vivo color rosso mentre il piumaggio della femmina tende al verde. Nidifica sugli alberi. La sua lunghezza raggiunge i sedici centimetri.

MINDRE KORSNÄBB: En bergsfågel som är 16 cm lång, och som sällan kommer ner på lågtliggande platser. Den livnär sig på fröna av olika slags tallar och granar, som växer i stora skogar i bergen i Grekland. På våren blir hanen skarpt röd, medan honan blir grönaktig. De bygger sina bon i träden.

KRUISBEK: Een bergvogel, die zelden naar laaggelegen gebieden komt. Hij voedt zich met de zaden van verschillende soorten naaldbomen, die als grote bossen in de Griekse bergen voorkomen. In de lente krijgt het mannetje een felrode kleur, terwijl het wijfje groenachtig wordt. Zij nestelen in bomen. Lengte 16 cm.

**36. Loxia
curvirostra.**

イスカ

低地にはめったに下りてこない山鳥。　山の多い北ギリシャの大きな森に生える種
々の松やモミの木の実をエサとする。　春には オスは 深い赤色を帯びるのに対し、
メスの羽毛は 緑に近くなる。　木の中に巣を作る。　体長 16cm。

CRETZCHMAR'S BUNTING: A migratory bird which visits Greece every summer. It lives in rocky scrub country or in open woodland. The female is light chestnut in colour with darker markings. The bunting feeds on seeds and measures 16 centimetres.

ΣΚΟΥΡΟΒΛΑΧΟΣ: Πουλί μεταναστευτικό πού ἔρχεται στήν ῾Ελλάδα κάθε καλοκαίρι. Ζεῖ σέ ἀνοιχτά πετρώδη μέρη, μέ θάμνους ἤ ἀραιά δένδρα. Τό θηλυκό ἔχει χρῶμα ἀνοιχτό καστανό μέ πιό σκοῦρα στίγματα. Τρέφεται μέ σπόρους. Μῆκος 16 ἑκ.

BRUANT CENDRILLARD: Oiseau migrateur qui vient en Grèce pour l'été. Il préfère les terrains pierreux et peu boisés. Le plumage de la femelle est châtain clair avec des tâches plus foncées. Il se nourrit de graines et mesure 16 cm.

GRAUER ORTOLAN: Zugvogel, der jeden Sommer nach Griechenland kommt. Er lebt in freigelegenen steinigen Gegenden mit Büschen und spärlichem Baumwuchs. Das weibliche Tier besitzt eine hellbraune (kastanienbraune) Färbung mit dunkleren Punkten. Der Vogel nährt sich von Samen. Seine Länge beträgt 16 cm.

ZIGOLO: Uccello migratore che viene in Grecia durante l'estate. Preferisce le regioni rocciose e sassose e poco boscose. Il piumaggio della femmina è castano chiaro con delle macchie più scure. Si ciba di semi e la sua lunghezza raggiunge i sedici centimetri.

MÖRK SPARV: Flyttfågel som kommer till Grekland varje sommar. De häckar på öppna klippiga platser, med buskar eller glesa träd. Honan har en ljus brun färg med mörkare fläckar. Den äter frön och mäter 16 cm.

BRUINKEELGORS: Een trekvogel, die elke zomer naar Griekenland komt. Hij leeft in schaarsbegroeide streken met struikgewas of verspreid staande bomen. Het wijfje is licht-kastanjebruin met donkerder plekken. Hij voedt zich met zaden. Lengte 16 cm.

37. Emberiza
caesia.

クレッチマーホウジロ

毎年夏になるとギリシャにやってくる渡り鳥。 岩の多いかん木地帯や、広々とした森
林に棲息する。 メスはこいもようを浮かべた明るい褐色をしている。 種子をエ
サとする。 体長16cm.

BLACK-HEADED BUNTING: This bird is 16 centimetres in length. It migrates to Greece from Asia every summer, and feeds on a variety of seeds and fruits, even including grapes. It lives on the plains, in scrub land or in open wooded areas. The female does not have the characteristic black head which gives the species its name, and its plumage tends to brown rather than yellow.

ΚΡΑΣΟΠΟΥΛΙ: Τό πουλί αὐτό ἔχει μῆκος 16 ἑκ. ῎Ερχεται ἀπό τήν ᾿Ασία κάθε καλοκαίρι. Τρέφεται μέ διάφορους σπόρους καί καρπούς καθώς καί μέ σταφύλια. Ζεῖ στίς πεδιάδες καί τούς θαμνότοπους ἤ σέ μέρη μέ ἀραιά δένδρα.

BRUANT MELANOCEPHALE: Cet oiseau mesurant 16 cm, vient de l'Asie pour l'été Il se nourrit de graines et de fruits, ainsi que de raisins. Il vit dans les plaines, le maquis et les regions peu boisées.

KAPPENAMMER: Dieser Vogel, der 16 cm lang ist, kommt jeden Sommer von Asien und nährt sich von verschiedenen Samen und Früchten sowie von Weintrauben. Er lebt in den Ebenen und an mit Büschen bestandenen Orten oder an Stellen mit spärlichem Baumbestand.

ZIGOLO MELANOCEFALE: Uccello migratore di una lunghezza di sedici centimetri, viene dall'Asia per trascorrere l'estate in Grecia. Si ciba di semi, di frutta e soprattutto di uva. Vive nelle pianure e nelle regioni poco boscose.

SVARTHUVAD SPARV: Denna fågel är 16 cm lång. Den kommer från Asien varje sommar. Den livnär sig på olika frön och bär, liksom på druvor. Den lever på slätterna och på buskmarker eller på platser med glest växande träd.

ZWARTKOPGORS: Deze 16 cm. lange vogel komt elke zomer uit Azië. Hij voedt zich met allerlei zaden en vruchten, waaronder druiven. Hij leeft in vlak land en in gebieden met struikgewas of met schaarse boomgroei.

38. Emberiza melanocephala.

クロアタマホウジロ

体長16cm。　毎夏アジアからギリシャに渡ってくる。　様々の種子や果物をエサとし、ブドウほでもついばむ。　平野やかん木地帯、広々とした森林地帯に棲息する。メスは名前のような特徴のある頭をしていない。　又、羽毛の色も、黄色というよりは茶に近い。

CIRL BUNTING: This bird is endemic to Greece. Length: 16 centimetres. The female is almost uniform in colour with some darker markings. It prefers open places or open woodland, and feeds on seeds.

ΣΙΡΛΟΤΣΙΧΛΟΝΟ: Πουλί ἐνδημικό στήν ˙Ελλάδα μέ μῆκος 16 ἐκ. Τό θηλυκό ἔχει χρῶμα ὁμοιόμορφο μέ στίγματα σκοῦρα. Προτιμᾶ τά ἀνοιχτά μέρη μέ ἀραιά δάση. Τρέφεται μέ σπόρους.

BRUANT ZIZI: Oiseau endémique en Grèce. La femelle est de couleur unie avec des tâches plus foncées. Il préfère les terrains presque nus, ou très peu boisés. Il se nourrit de graines et mesure 16 cm.

ZAUNAMMER: Ein in Griechenland auftretender Zugvogel von 16 cm Länge. Das weibliche Tier besitzt eine gleichmäßige Färbung mit dunkleren Punkten. Das Tier bevorzugt die offen gelegenen Plätze mit spärlichem Baumwuchs. Es nährt sich von Samen.

ZIGOLO NERO: Uccello endemico in Grecia. La femmina è monocolore con delle macchie più scure. Preferisce i terreni spogli o pochissimo boscosi. Si ciba di semi e raggiunge la lunghezza di sedici centimetri.

SPARV: En inhemsk fågel i Grekland, med en längd av 16 cm. Honan har en jämn färg med mörka fläckar. Den föredrar öppna platser med gles skog. Livnär sig på frön.

CIRLGORS: Een in Griekenland inheemse vogel. Het wijfje is egaal van kleur met donkere vlekken. Deze vogel heeft voorkeur voor open terrein met schaarse boomgroei. Zaden vormen zijn voedsel. Lengte 16 cm.

**39. Emberiza
cirlus.**

シルルホウジロ

キリシャ特有の鳥で体長16cm。　メスは全身ほとんど同色で、こいもようが少しばかりついているだけである。　広々とした場所や森林を好み、種子をエサとする。

DUNNOCK: A northern bird which migrates to Greece only in the winter, the dunnock is 15 centimetres in length. It inhabits the plains and scrub land, where it feeds on various insects.

ΘΑΜΝΟΨΑΛΤΗΣ: Πουλί τοῦ βορρᾶ πού στήν Ἑλλάδα κατεβαίνει μόνο τό χειμώνα. Ἔχει μῆκος 15 ἑκ. Τρέφεται μέ ἔντομα. Ζεῖ στίς πεδιάδες καί τούς θαμνότοπους.

ACCENTEUR MOUCHET: Oiseau nordique qui vient en Grèce seulement pour y passer l'hiver. Il mesure 15 cm. et se nourrit d'insectes. Il vit dans les plaines et le maquis.

HECKENBRAUNELLE: Ein Vogel aus dem Norden, der nur im Winter nach Griechenland herunterzieht. Er ist 15 cm land und nährt sich von Insekten. Er lebt in den Ebenen und an mit Büschen bestandenen Orten.

ACCENTORICO: Uccello settentrionale che migra in Grecia per trascorrere l'inverno. Si ciba di insetti e la sua lunghezza raggiunge i quindici centimetri. Vive nelle pianure.

JÄRNSPARV: En fågel från norr, som flyttar ner till Grekland endast på vintern. Den är 15 cm lång. Den livnär sig på insekter. Den lever på slätter och i buskvegetation.

HEGGEMUS: Een vogel uit Noord-Europa, die alleen 's winters naar Griekenland trekt. Zijn voedsel bestaat uit insecten. Hij leeft in de vlakten en in gebieden met laag gewas. Lengte 15 cm.

**40. Prunella
modularis.**

イワヒバリ

冬にのみギリシャに渡ってくる北の鳥で，体長15cm。 種々の昆虫をエサとし，平野
やかん木地帯に住む。